SERIES EDITOR: SYDNEY WOOD

*Understanding*
**People in the Past**

# A Separate Kingdom

## FINLAY MCKICHAN

Hodder & Stoughton
A MEMBER OF THE HODDER HEADLINE GROUP

# INTRODUCTION

This is a history book. It helps you to know more about people's lives in the past. It helps you to see how life changed then, and how it has changed since. It shows you WHAT happened in the past, WHEN, HOW and WHY we think it happened.

This book uses two kinds of dates - years and centuries. A century is a hundred years long. We count them from the year Jesus Christ was born. So 1314 (the year the Battle of Bannockburn was fought) is a fourteenth century date.

All the people in this book lived in Scotland between the eleventh and the fifteenth centuries. This time is called The Middle Ages. This means it is between early times and modern times. We use the word medieval for people who lived in the Middle Ages.

You will find out how medieval Scots lived and how they died. Sometimes their lives were very different from yours. Sometimes they are surprisingly the same. You will discover how Scotland became one country and how its people came to think of themselves as Scots. You will learn about famous people (like William Wallace) whom Scots today still like to hear about in stories and films. You will find out about these from pictures and writing which were done at the time. You will see photographs of things which were made in the Middle Ages (such as pots and jugs). You may see these things in your local museum. You will discover that there are still many medieval buildings (such as castles and churches). Many of these are kept in good repair so that we can see them and remember the Middle Ages.

# Contents

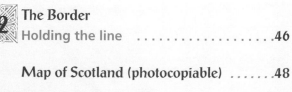

# Who Lived in Scotland 1000 Years Ago?

The country we now call Scotland was very different a thousand years ago, at the beginning of the eleventh century. Different peoples lived in each part of it.

They had their own rulers, and they all spoke different languages. If you could travel back in time and interview them, this is what they might say:

▼ **Source 1**

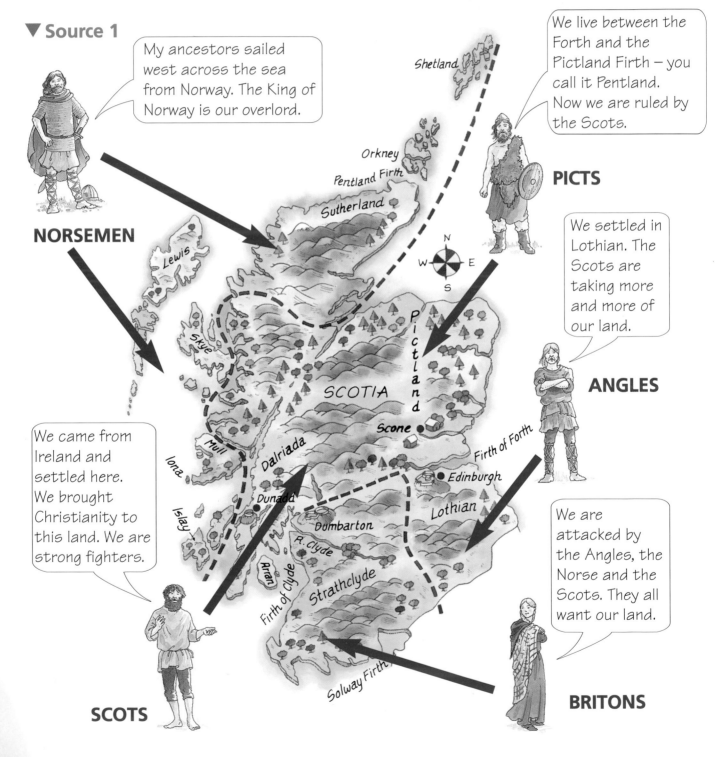

My ancestors sailed west across the sea from Norway. The King of Norway is our overlord.

**NORSEMEN**

We live between the Forth and the Pictland Firth – you call it Pentland. Now we are ruled by the Scots.

**PICTS**

We settled in Lothian. The Scots are taking more and more of our land.

**ANGLES**

We came from Ireland and settled here. We brought Christianity to this land. We are strong fighters.

**SCOTS**

We are attacked by the Angles, the Norse and the Scots. They all want our land.

**BRITONS**

4

▼ **Source 2**

> I am a farmer, but I still know how to use a sword. Sometimes we get the boats out to raid the Scots. Their churches are full of gold.

> We are forgetting our own language. More and more of us speak the language of the Scots. You call it Gaelic.

**A PICT**
We Picts are Christians. A holy man called Columba taught us about Christ. The Scots defeated us. They rule us now.

**A NORSEMAN**
We speak Norwegian. I live in the southern land, which you call Sutherland. Sometimes we fight for the King of Norway.

> We speak our own Angle-ish language. Lots of people in the Lowlands now speak it. You call it English.

**AN ANGLE**
We have built forts to guard against the Scots, but we cannot keep them out. They have taken over a lot of our land.

> Our language is Gaelic. Many people speak Gaelic now. We are Christians and our patron saint is the blessed Columba.

> The Scots and the Norse would like to take over our land. So we often have to fight them.

**A SCOT**
We came from Ireland about 500 years ago. We call our land Dalriada. You call it Argyll. We defeated the Picts, so now Dalriada and Pictland are one new land. It is called Scotia.

**A BRITON**
The Angles have pushed us back into Strathclyde. Our capital is on top of the Rock of Dumbarton. This means Fort of the Britons.

# 2 How Do We Know About Them?

All the peoples who once lived in Scotland have left something behind. Some left buildings or beautiful carvings. Some left precious jewellery or games. Some left their special language or their religion.

## Source 1 ▶

The Norsemen played a game like our game of chess. Here is one of their chess pieces, made of walrus tusk. It was found in Lewis in the Hebrides. It shows a Norseman dressed for battle.

This chess piece is called The Berserker. A Berserker was a Norse warrior who fought furiously in battle. Do you know a modern word like this? What does it mean?

## ◀ Source 2

The Picts put up stones with carved pictures on them. One of these stones shows Picts on horseback fighting fiercely.

## ▲ Source 3

The Scots used to crown their kings at a fort on a hill called Dunadd. On top of Dunadd is a rock, which you can see here. A hole has been cut in it just big enough for a man to place his foot. The kings did this when they were crowned. It showed that they were stepping into the shoes of the great kings of the past.

CONSTANTINE K. AND M. FOVNDER OF GOVAN CHVRCH ✛ A.D. 576 PRESERVED WITHIN THE

## ▲ Source 4

The Britons had to fight hard against the Scots and the Norse. Their warriors were often in battle. When they were not fighting they hunted deer. This picture shows a carving on a stone coffin This sort of coffin is called a sarcophagus.

## ▼ Source 5

The Angles used to own all the land through Lothian to the Forth. Their King Edwin set up a fort there to guard against the Picts. It was named after him - Edinburgh. Why was it a good place to build a fort? Did it save the Angles from the Scots?

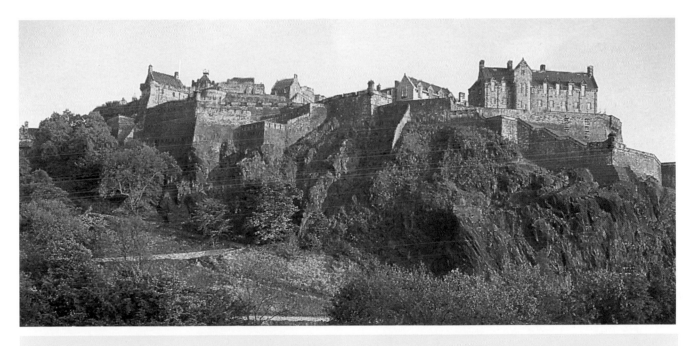

1 Copy the map on page 48. Write on it all the places shown on the map on page 2. Now put a big spot on the map in the place where you live.

2 Now imagine that you were born in the eleventh century. Write about your life then. Who would be your friends? Who would be your enemies?

## A C T I V I T I E S

# A Warrior and a Queen

We are now in the eleventh century. The Scots have a very strong King, called Malcolm. His nickname is Canmore, which means great chief. He often invades England to try to win new lands. The English fear him and think he is very cruel. Malcolm is married to Margaret. Her grandfather was once King of England. In 1066, Normans from France took over England, and Margaret and her family had to escape. They sailed to Scotland and Malcolm gave them shelter.

## ▼ Source 1

This is what an English monk wrote about one of Malcolm's raids:

> *Some old men and women were beheaded with swords and others were stuck with spears like pigs being killed for eating.*

## ▼ Source 2

This is the bay where Margaret's ship anchored when she came to ask Malcolm for help. Ever since then it has been called Margaret's Hope.

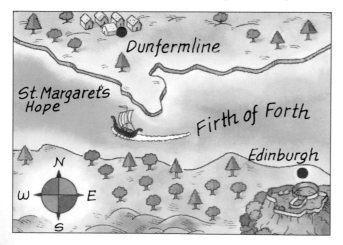

## ▲ Source 3

This picture shows Malcolm going to meet Margaret when she arrived in Scotland. It was painted in about 1900 on a wall in the Scottish National Portrait Gallery in Edinburgh.

King Malcolm married Margaret in 1069 and she became Queen of Scots. Queen Margaret had lived in Hungary and England. She brought with her many new ideas. We know about them because her priest, called Turgot, wrote her life story. This is what he said:

> *She ordered precious goods from different countries. When the Scots saw them they bought new clothes of different colours. Gold and silver were now used in the royal palace for the wall hangings and for the cups and plates used at table.*

▲ **Source 4**

Margaret was very religious. Turgot the priest says she spent many hours praying. The Queen brought her children up strictly. She told them it was very important to worship God, and to have fine churches and holy churchmen. People thought Queen Margaret was so holy that she was made a saint after she died.

**Source 5** ▶
This is a picture of St Matthew from a book of gospels. It was probably used by Queen Margaret. All books had to be written and painted by hand in those days. Why?

Read Source 4 again. Imagine you are Margaret's priest, Turgot. Write the story of her life. If you like, you can make your paper look old by colouring it with a teabag soaked in cold water. Make sure the paper is completely dry before you start writing on it.

**A C T I V I T I E S**

▲ **Source 6**
Here is Saint Margaret's Chapel in Edinburgh Castle. It was built by Margaret's son, David. He wanted people to remember his mother for ever.

SCS MATTHEUS EVANGELISTA

# David - Maker of Scotland
## 1124-1153

King David was the son of Malcolm and Margaret. He was determined to make Scotland safer and stronger than ever. He worked out new ways of making sure that his orders were carried out. He set up special royal towns and abbeys all over Scotland. His royal towns were called burghs. He gave land to strong knights who would fight for him.

◀ **Source 1**
This picture of David was drawn to show what a strong king he was. It was made only about six years after he died, so it probably shows what he really looked like.

I am David, King of Scotland, son of King Malcolm and Queen Margaret. I want to make Scotland rich, strong and peaceful.

I have set up royal burghs with markets. People must come to them to buy and sell their goods. I promise to protect them, and they pay me taxes.

My new Scottish churches are very special. They are called abbeys. Monks live there. They are good men who praise God. The abbeys are very beautiful - just like the abbeys of England and France.

I have given land to powerful Norman and English knights. They promise to obey me and to help me in battle against my enemies. They are building castles to protect my land.

▲ **Source 2**

**Source 3** ▶

Jedburgh Abbey cost David a lot of money to build. It is built of stone. The builders were called masons. They came from England to work there. The Scottish abbeys had arches, pillars and carvings as beautiful as the ones in France and England. The monks who lived in the abbeys knew how to worship God in the most modern ways.

▼ **Source 4**

> I am the Abbot of Jedburgh. King David is a good Christian. My monks pray for his soul.

> I am Mary. My husband Robert sells cloth in Edinburgh. He has to pay taxes to King David.

> My name is De Morville. I am a Norman lord from England. King David has given me land. My knights will fight for him whenever he asks.

> I am Lady De Morville. We have built a strong castle here.

> I am Robert. I am a merchant from the royal burgh of Edinburgh. King David has organised things well for us.

**Get into a group. Each person decides to be one of the people in Source 4. Explain to each other why you obey King David's orders.**

**A C T I V I T I E S**

# 5

# De Morville's New Castle

Like all the new Norman lords, De Morville has built his castle on top of a huge pile of earth, called a motte. He can see out clearly for miles around. He keeps his animals and stores his food lower down the slope, in a place called the bailey. In time of danger, the local people come in, and then De Morville's men defend everybody.

▼ Source 1

The drawbridges can be pulled up shut if the fort is attacked.

This wooden fencing is called a stockade. It protects the tower.

The lord and his most important people live in this wooden tower.

This is the bailey. Bailey means an enclosed space. Food and animals are stored here. This is where the lord's servants live and work.

This rounded pile of earth is the motte. It is a French word. It means mound.

De Morville can send soldiers out from his castle to keep order anywhere on his lands. One day, the King may decide to set up a royal burgh and a church here. The shopkeepers and the priest will be very important. They are certain to tell people to obey De Morville and King David.

### ◄ Source 2

This is how one of the Norman castles looks today. Only the motte is left. The wooden tower and stockade have gone - perhaps they were set on fire long ago. Or perhaps they rotted away. The people moved away to live somewhere else.

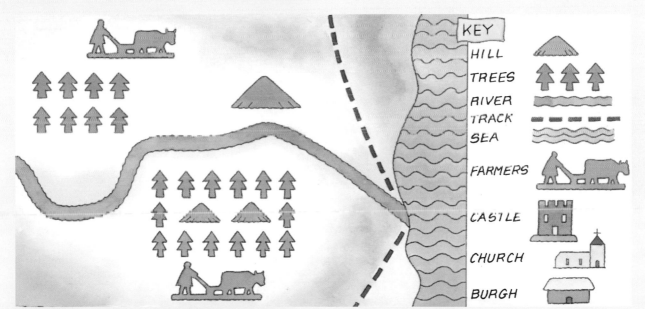

KEY
HILL
TREES
RIVER
TRACK
SEA
FARMERS
CASTLE
CHURCH
BURGH

Imagine you are a Norman lord. King David has given you some land. He has ordered you to set up a castle, royal burgh and church. This map shows what your land looked like when you arrived.

Copy this map, and mark where you will build your castle, the burgh and the church. Write notes explaining why.

Think about these things:

- Is it better to have a castle on a hill or on flat land? What will you build it with? Are the materials close by? What will you drink and where will you get it?

- The burgh needs to be easy to reach. People will bring their goods by track, river and sea.

- As many people as possible must be able to walk to the church.

## A C T I V I T I E S

# Working the Land

**6**

Most medieval Scots were farmers. They could not read or write. And the people who could read and write did not think that farmers were important. So they did not tell us much about them.

Archaeologists found a medieval township at Rattray, near Peterhead. It was owned in medieval times by the Comyn family.

> Today, people called archaeologists can find out about the past. They are like time detectives. They find things left by people in the past. From these they can work out how people lived.

▼ **Source 1**

This picture has been drawn by a modern artist from clues found at Rattray. Let us imagine that it is rented by one of Comyn's farmers.

yard to keep pigs (for eating)

hay stacks to feed horse

barn for storing corn to make bread

the horse carries things and pulls the plough

hens give eggs and m...

house made of wood and clay with hole in roof for smoke from...

vegetable ground for cabbages

peat for the fire

water barrel to catch rain

> I do not have far to walk to my land. I share it with the other farmers here. It is split up into wide strips. In each strip the soil is piled up to the middle. The best land is nearest the houses. The sheep and cattle graze the land further away.
>
> I grow oats and barley. I sell some of my produce to get money. I need this to pay the land rent to Comyn.

### ◀ Source 2

These medieval farmers are ploughing. Four oxen are pulling the plough. Can you see the sharp cutter on the plough? It breaks into the soil. Behind the cutter there is a board. It pushes the soil to one side and digs a long hole, called a furrow. That is where the seed is planted. Why do you think one of the farmers has a whip?

### ◀ Source 3

These farmers are cutting the ripe corn. They are using a special knife, called a sickle. How would you feel if you had to cut corn all day like this?

### ◀ Source 4

These people want the grains from the corn. One man is hitting the corn to loosen the corn grains. The other man is shaking the corn in the basket, so all the bits fly away. Only the good grain is left. What do you think they will make from the corn?

1 Imagine you are one of Comyn's farmers, or a farmer's wife. You are showing a visitor round the farm. Tell your visitor about the buildings, tools and animals.

2 Comyn wants to put up your rent. You cannot pay more. You must tell Comyn why. Perhaps the weather has been bad? Have you had a new baby? Are you not well?

## ACTIVITIES

# The Idea of Scotland

David was a strong king of the Scots. But most people living in the country still thought of themselves as men or women of Galloway or Buchan or Lothian. After David died there was a lot of fighting. It took a hundred years before people everywhere thought of themselves as Scots. How did this happen?

▼ **Source 1**

**1** After David died, the Kings of the Scots called in more Norman lords to keep order.

**2** The lords now built their castles of stone. They were much harder to attack.

**3** Again and again the kings of the Scots led armies into battle. They fought their enemies in the north and south west, and the West Highlands and Islands.

One of the most important battles was at Largs in 1263. The Scots King Alexander III at last defeated the Norsemen of the West Highlands and Islands.

◀ **Source 2**

This fourteenth century coin was called a **gold lion.** It reminded the Scots of their King and country. On one side is a lion, which is the coat of arms of the Scottish kings. When the lion stands up like this, it is called a **lion rampant.** On the other side of the coin is a picture of St Andrew on his cross. This type of cross is called a **saltire.** Where else do you see it?

**4** In 1266, Alexander III met messengers from the King of Norway at Perth. The Norwegians agreed to give up the Western Isles to Scotland. They kept only Orkney and Shetland.

**5** Scottish soldiers now go into battle with the flag of a new patron saint - Saint Andrew. Some Scots still look up to Saint Columba. But they all feel united by Saint Andrew.

**6** The largest church in Scotland was built to the memory of Saint Andrew. It is in the place named after him. People came from all over the country to worship there.

**1** Draw or paint a banner showing things which made people in the thirteenth century proud to be Scots.

**2** Make a list and draw pictures of other things today which make people feel proud that they are Scottish.

A C T I V I T I E S

# The Builders of Glasgow Cathedral

Glasgow Cathedral was built in the thirteenth century. Today, it is kept in good order with money from the taxes we pay. We can find clues in the cathedral which tell us about life in medieval times.

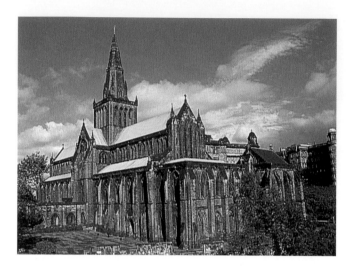

## Source 1 ▶

Most of this end of Glasgow Cathedral was built on the orders of William Bondington. He was Bishop of Glasgow from 1233 to 1258. Building the cathedral was as big a task as building a motorway today.

Imagine that Bishop Bondington is telling us why he did it:

When I started to rebuild the cathedral I knew it would take many years and all the money I could find. I may not live to see all the work done. Why do I do it? It is the largest building in the West of Scotland and can be seen from a long way away.

I am not doing this so that people will remember me. It is to show how much I and the people of Glasgow love God.

Of course I am sure that I will go to heaven because I have done this. The lords who have put up some of the money believe that, too. That is very important to us.

You must understand that for us life can end very suddenly. I may fall sick and die next year - or even next week. I need to be sure that God will be good to me after I leave this life.

▲ **Source 2**

# • William Bondington's dream •

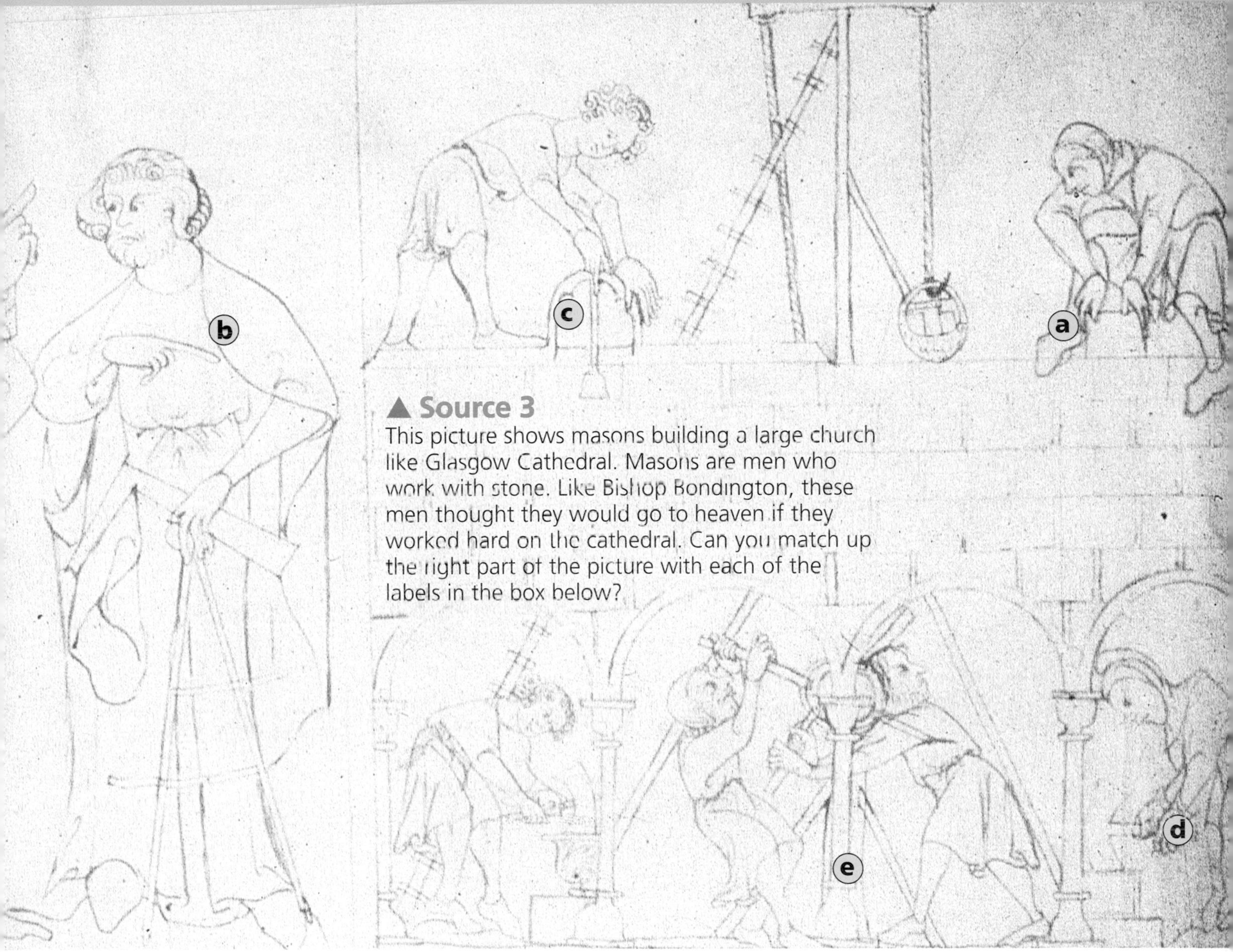


**▲ Source 3**

This picture shows masons building a large church like Glasgow Cathedral. Masons are men who work with stone. Like Bishop Bondington, these men thought they would go to heaven if they worked hard on the cathedral. Can you match up the right part of the picture with each of the labels in the box below?

**1. The master mason designed the building. He is explaining what is being done. He has a compass to measure and draw circles and arches. He has a set square to make his corners and lines straight.**

**2. This mason is cutting the stones.**

**3. These men are working hard to turn the hoist which lifts the stones.**

**4. This mason is fitting the stones in place.**

**5. This mason has a tool for checking that the wall is level.**

Answers: a=4; b=1; c=5; d=2; e=3

# Troubled Times

King Alexander III died very suddenly one night in 1286. The nobles and people of Scotland were worried. Alexander had no son. Who would be their next King?

In medieval times, there were no newspapers, TV or radio. People told each other the news. Imagine that you are hearing this story one evening round the fire in your house for the first time:

**Source 1 ▼**

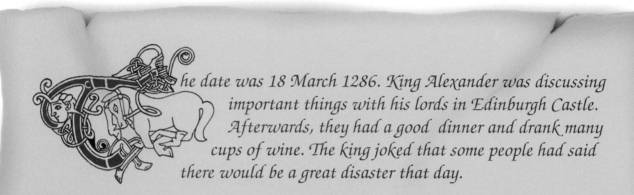

The date was 18 March 1286. King Alexander was discussing important things with his lords in Edinburgh Castle. Afterwards, they had a good dinner and drank many cups of wine. The king joked that some people had said there would be a great disaster that day.

Some of the lords did not laugh. A wild wind was blowing. Rain and snow showers swept past the castle windows. The dark came early. They thought this was a sign that something terrible would happen.

The king was not worried. He left on horseback after dark. He wanted to ride back to Kinghorn to see his wife. He was used to riding around Scotland through the night in all weathers.

He had to cross the Firth of Forth. The ferryman warned him that it was dangerous. "Are you afraid to die with me?" the King asked the ferryman. "There is no-one I would rather die with," said the ferryman. And he took the King across.

When Alexander came to the burgh of Inverkeithing, a man he knew said to him "Lord, what are you doing here in such weather? I have warned you that your night journeys are dangerous. Stay the night at my house!" But the King refused. He rode off and asked two men to walk with him and show him the way.

Somewhere in the dark and noise of the storm the King lost the two guides. Perhaps they could not keep up with him. Suddenly, Alexander's horse slipped and fell on a cliff. Alexander plunged down onto the rocks by the seashore. His body was found there the next morning.

## Source 2 ▼ What happened after King Alexander died?

**1** "We must keep Scotland for Queen Margaret."

Alexander's grand-daughter Margaret was to be the next Queen. She was a young girl living in Norway with her father and mother, the King and Queen of Norway.

**2** In 1290 when Margaret was ten, she set off for Scone to be crowned, but she died in Orkney. There were no near relatives of Alexander left. The closest were Robert Bruce and John Balliol.

**3** "John Balliol's family is closest to King Alexander."

The lords asked King Edward I of England to choose either Robert or John to be the next king of the Scots. First Edward forced the Scots to accept him as their lord. Then he chose John Balliol.

**4** "Tell King John I order him to London!"

John was crowned King of Scots in 1292. Most people agreed that John was closest to King Alexander. Edward soon showed that he really meant to be John's lord and send him orders.

**1** Work in a group. One of you is King Alexander III. The rest are all the other people he meets on the 18th March, 1286. Act out what you think happened that day.

**2** Make a wall display showing the things that caused the Scots lords to ask King Edward to decide who should be the next King of Scots. (Clue: Look again at the report on page 20 and the first two pictures above.)

## A C T I V I T I E S

# William Wallace

William Wallace died 700 years ago. But people still remember him today. William Wallace is important because he made the Scots believe that Scotland should be a separate country. People all over Scotland have put up monuments to William Wallace. They want to show that they think he is a great man.

In 1296 King Edward I of England invaded Scotland and captured King John. He took away John's crown. He also took the stone of Scone on which Scots kings had been crowned for over 300 years. He moved it to Westminster Abbey, in London, where it can still be seen.

Edward called all the Scots lords and knights to Berwick and told them he was now ruler of Scotland. He sent English soldiers to man every important Scottish castle. English officials, called sheriffs, were in charge of every Scottish town.

William Wallace did not accept Edward as his lord.

**Source 1 ▶**
Monuments to William Wallace have been put up in many parts of Scotland. This one is a statue in the centre of Aberdeen.

He believed Scotland should be a separate country. William Wallace was remembered as a very strong man. A poet called Blind Harry wrote a poem 150 years later, and said he was:

*Strong and handsome to see; his brows were hard, his arms were long and thick.*

▲ **Source 2**

▲ **Source 3**
The National Wallace Monument is a tall tower on a hill near Stirling. You can visit it to see a display which shows what Wallace did.

English soldiers murdered Wallace's wife, and so in revenge he killed the Sheriff of Lanark. He escaped to the forest of Ettrick in the Borders.

There Wallace gathered soldiers around him. They attacked the English whenever they could. Andrew Murray, son of a great lord, did the same in northern Scotland.

By summer 1297, they had driven most of the English home. While they were attacking English soldiers at Dundee, they heard that a large English army was marching towards Stirling. They hurried south to try to defeat it.

**Source 4** ▼
Nowadays at Scone only a copy of the real Stone can be seen.

When Wallace and Murray reached Stirling Bridge they saw a huge English army. There were 500 knights on horseback and 10,000 foot soldiers.

But Wallace knew he could trick the enemy. The English had to cross the bridge to attack the Scots. It was narrow and made of wood.

The Scots watched until about half the English soldiers were across the bridge. Then Wallace gave the order to attack.

## ▼ Source 1

The Scots attacked the English when they were half way across Stirling bridge. The front of the English army turned back and crashed into the rest of the men and horses.

1 Make up a Song about why Wallace is remembered in Scotland. Choose a well-known Scottish tune that you like. Make up your own words to it.

2 You are an old man or woman. Tell your grandchildren about the time you or your husband fought with Wallace at Stirling Bridge.

ACTIVITIES

The Scots fought fiercely. Men were shouting and horses neighing. English soldiers and their horses fell into the river and were drowned.

Then the Scots set fire to the bridge, and the rest of the English soldiers fled. After the battle, Wallace wrote:

*Scotland, thanks be to God, is recovered from the English.*

▲ Source 2

But the English came back next year. They brought archers who could hit the Scots from far away. There was a battle at Falkirk, and now the English won.

In 1305 the English found Wallace and took him to London. They said he was a traitor. He said he had never accepted King Edward as his lord. So he could not be a traitor. He was hanged and while he was still alive, his insides were torn out.

Parts of his body were sent to different Scottish towns as a warning. But this did not frighten the Scots. They were determined to carry on the struggle he had begun.

▲ Source 3
Wallace was hanged in London in 1305. His head was stuck on a pole on London Bridge.

# Attacking a Stone Castle

In the thirteenth century, the king and his lords began to build castles of stone. They were easier to defend than wooden ones. It often took months to capture a stone castle. The enemy camped outside and kept attacking. This was called a siege.

### ▼ Source 1
This picture was drawn in about 1316. It shows Carlisle Castle holding out against the Scots.

**Crossbows were slow to use. You had to wind them back with a kind of wheel before you could shoot the arrow.**

**Big metal hat protects against arrows.**

**This knight kills the catapult man with his lance.**

**CATAPULT**

**The soldier will cut the rope with his axe. The stone will fly out at the castle wall and make a hole in it.**

**Pick-axes can cut holes in the bottom of the castle wall and make tunnels.**

**SCALING LADDER**

**The man on the ladder is trying to climb over the castle wall. But he cannot do it. Why? Sometimes the men on the castle wall fought so hard that often the ladders - and the men on them - fell flat to the ground.**

**▲ Source 2**
Bothwell Castle near Glasgow was built at the end of the thirteenth century. The rich lord who built it wanted to be sure it could not be captured. The huge tower is over 30 metres high. The walls are five metres thick!

**▲ Source 3**
The English King Edward I attacked Bothwell. He built a huge wooden tower, called a siege tower. Edward captured the castle within a month. Can you say how he did it?

**Source 4 ▶**
This picture shows new parts added to Bothwell Castle to make it even more difficult to attack. Look at the stonework. The lower parts are made of big blocks. They slope outwards. Why would this make it difficult to cut through the wall? The tower had ledges at the top. Soldiers could lean out over their attackers. What would they do?

1 Work in a group. One of you is leading the siege of Bothwell Castle. Discuss with your knights how you will capture it.

   Make a list of the things you will order the knights to do, and when. Your knights must then draw pictures to show their soldiers what to do.

2 Is there a medieval castle near where you live? Find out how it kept attackers out. Discuss with your teacher and your group or class which sources you will use. Try different sources: books in school or in the library; leaflets in the tourist office; pictures and objects in the museum. Talk about what you discover.

**A C T I V I T I E S**

# Robert Bruce

After the battle of Falkirk, English armies kept coming to Scotland. They captured more and more castles and lands. The Scots did not stop fighting, but it looked as if they might lose. But in 1306 Robert Bruce was crowned King of Scots at Scone. To help him become King, he had murdered his rival, John Comyn. So Comyn's family and supporters started to fight Bruce.

Soon after he was crowned, Robert was defeated by his enemies and had to escape from the mainland for a time. Now he never risked a full battle against the English. He ambushed their soldiers and then hurried away before he could be caught. When he captured a castle, he knocked down the walls to put it out of action. Sometimes he was cruel. He killed people and animals and burned the houses and crops in Buchan.

In 1314, the English were going to attack Stirling Castle. Robert took a great risk and decided to face them with a full Scottish army. On the first day, the Scots stopped the English getting past them to reach the castle. As Robert was fighting, he was attacked by Sir Henry de Bohun.

A poet called John Barbour wrote a poem about this 50 years later. He said:

> Sir Henry missed the noble King!
> The King stood up in his stirrups and lifted his axe, so sharp and good. He aimed such a mighty stroke that Sir Henry's skull was almost cut through.

▲ Source 2

**Source 1 ▶**
Robert Bruce spent much of his time fighting. This statue at Bannockburn shows him in knight's armour, on a warhorse.

**Source 3 ▶**
The English King Edward I is marching into this Scottish castle.

Look carefully at this map. It shows where the armies were on the morning of the second day. Which do you think was in the best position? To help you decide, think about these things:

- Is a marsh easy to walk or run or fight in?

- Would you feel safe with a marsh behind you?

- Would you feel safe to have a river with steep banks behind you?

- Would you feel safe with high ground behind you?

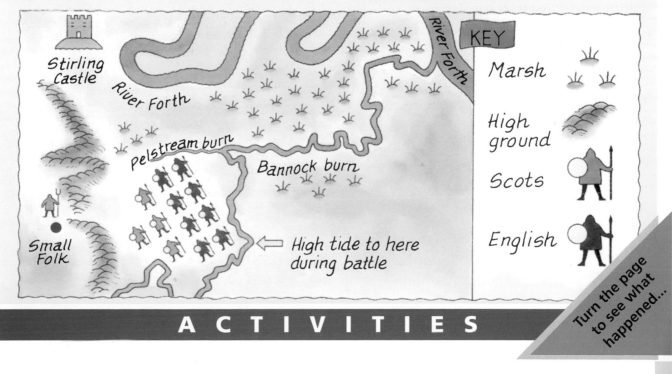

Stirling Castle

River Forth

River Forth

Pelstream burn

Bannock burn

Small Folk

High tide to here during battle

**KEY**

Marsh

High ground

Scots

English

**A C T I V I T I E S**

Turn the page to see what happened...

# The Battle of Bannockburn 1314

Robert's army had 5500 men. The English King Edward II had 20 000. Robert thought about leading his army away during the night. But a Scottish knight came across from the English side to Robert's side. He said, "My lord king, now is the time, if you ever mean to win Scotland. The English have lost heart after the hard fighting yesterday."

And so Robert decided to stay and fight. He made a great speech to his men before the battle. John Barbour the poet tells us that Robert said:

> "The Scots have a great advantage. We fight for our lives, for our children, for our wives and for the freedom of our land."

▲ Source 1

The Scots moved forward first. Then they stopped and knelt. John Barbour tells the rest of the story:

> The English king said 'They kneel for mercy'. But an English lord who knew the Scots replied 'They ask for mercy, but not from you. They are praying to God. These men will win or die.'

▲ Source 2

The Scottish spearmen attacked the English knights. Follow the numbers in Source 3 to find out what happened.

Source 3 ▶

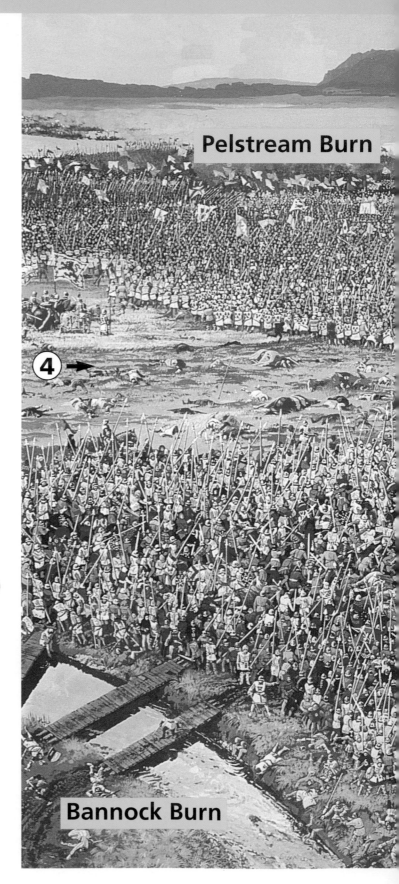

Pelstream Burn

④→

Bannock Burn

**③ Stirling Castle**

1. The Scots were mostly soldiers on foot with spears. When they were attacked, they made a **hedgehog** with their spears pointing out.

2. The English had about 2000 knights on horseback. But they could not break the Scottish hedgehogs. The English knights were squeezed between the Scots and Bannock and Pelstream burns. They began to panic, and many of them drowned as they tried to escape.

3. King Edward II knew he had lost the battle. He tried to shelter in Stirling Castle, but the Scots were too close and he had to ride to Dunbar and take a small boat to England.

4. At the back of King Robert's army were some men who were not proper soldiers, just ordinary people or **small folk.** These small folk now rushed from this direction to attack. The English thought another Scottish army had arrived, and they fled.

You are either:

**a** one of the men who were the **small folk** of Robert's army. You are celebrating in a tavern after the battle.

Or:

**b** the wife of one of the **small folk** of Robert's army. Your husband has come home after the battle.

*Tell the story of the battle to the people around you.*

**A C T I V I T I E S**

1 These sources show you what people thought of Robert Bruce while he was alive and after he was dead. Look carefully at these pages and look back at pages 28-31. What do you think of Robert? Write down your reasons. What do the other people in your group think?

2 Make a seal with modelling clay showing Robert as a warrior king.

## ACTIVITIES

### Source 1 ▶

A sixteenth century artist painted this picture of Robert and his wife, about 200 years after Robert died. Look at what he is wearing. What does this tell you about how people in the sixteenth century saw Robert?

*He took risks to encourage his men. So he was often successful even when things seemed very difficult.*

### ◀ Source 2

John Barbour wrote these words in his poem 'The Bruce' in the 1360s. Do you think Barbour thought Robert was a good king?

### ◀ Source 3

This was one of Robert's seals. A seal was a way of signing a letter or a law. It showed the king approved. The seal was pressed into hot wax to make a picture. Why do you think kings and lords used seals instead of signing their names? (Clue: Some of them were unable to do something you can do). On this seal, Robert decided to show himself sitting on a throne. He is not wearing his armour. Perhaps he is making new laws. Why did he want people to see him like this?

### ▲ Source 4

The Scots lords wrote this letter in 1320. It says why they support King Robert. It is called the Declaration of Arbroath. Each lord has added a ribbon with a wax circle on it. What do you think these wax circles are?

### ▼ Source 5

This is what the Declaration of Arbroath says. What do the lords think Robert has already done? What must he go on doing to keep their support? What effect did all the fighting have on the way Scots thought about themselves and the English?

*No one who did not live through it can describe the killings, theft and fire brought to Scotland by King Edward. But at last it pleased God to allow King Robert to give us back our freedom. To do this he cheerfully suffered exhaustion and danger. But if he ever allows us to be ruled by the king or people of England, we will at once try to throw him out and make a new king.*

*As long as a hundred of us remain alive we will never agree to be ruled by the English. We do not fight for glory or riches or honour, but for freedom alone, which no honest man will lose but with his life.*

# Life in a Castle

It is the fourteenth century. You are a traveller. You have been invited to join Lord De Morville for dinner. The De Morvilles have built themselves a stone castle. It is much more welcoming than the wooden one of 200 years before.

You know you will get a good meal. You ask to see the meal being cooked. A servant takes you down into the huge kitchens.

## ▲ Source 1

De Morville's kitchen looks like this. Can you see these things:

- a cook pounding meat to make it tender
- a cook mixing pastry
- two small pots cooking on the fire - one for soup, one for stew
- a big pot with lots of different things cooking in it - all together!
- ducks roasting on a spit. Why are the people with long spoons pouring fat on? What is the little boy in the corner doing? Why?

## Source 2 ▶

A servant shows you into the castle hall. You will sit at the end of one of the tables in the picture. Musicians are playing harps and horns. You are a long way from the fire. What is hanging on the walls? And why are you glad to see them? You are a long way from the lord. Can you see him? What is special about where he is sitting? Who is sitting beside him?

The people at your table are the knights who live in the castle and fight for the lord. The lord's priest is there, too. Important servants (like the farm manager) also sit here.

Work in a group. Decide who will be the lord, lady, servant and visitor. Then act out the conversation during an evening at De Morville's Castle. The visitor will have news from far away. Have the English caused any trouble? Has anyone met the king?

The people at the castle will be proud of their home and their food. Has the harvest been good this year? What other visitors have been to the castle? What news did they bring?

## ACTIVITIES

### Source 3 ▶
Lots of things cook together inside the big pot. There are eggs, vegetables, bacon and puddings. What does this taste like?

### ▼ Source 6
After enjoying the food and wine, you visit the toilet. This is what it is like. It hangs over the outside of the castle wall. What do you think about this?

### ◀ Source 4
This is a metal jug, called a ewer. It holds water to pour over your hands. Why do you have to do this? (Look back at Source 2).

### Source 5 ▶
Some people are gambling in a quiet side room. But you decide to play this game. What is it? (Clue: look at page 6).

# The Townspeople of Aberdeen

Imagine you are going to visit the houses in the picture on page 37. Children from Aberdeen schools can do this. They can step into medieval Aberdeen, because the people at the Art Gallery have rebuilt a house just like the one here.

▼ **Source 1**
School parties can visit a house just like the ones in Medieval Aberdeen.

You may be surprised to learn that a modern shopping centre helped to show how people lived in medieval Aberdeen. Buildings were knocked down to make way for the new centre. When the ground was clear, archaeologists were able to dig down. They found clues about the first houses here and the people who lived in them. From these clues the archaeologists could rebuild a medieval house.

The houses had fireplaces made of stones. The fireplace was in the middle of the floor and there was no proper chimney. People must have coughed a lot as the smoke swirled round the house.

Many houses in medieval Aberdeen were not on the main streets. They were on strips of land running back from the street. They are called 'backland' houses.

**▼ Source 2**
This shows the small backland houses and the large houses on the main street. Can you say what all the people are doing? Compare it to your life at home today.

The archaeologists in Aberdeen had to work fast so that they did not delay the builders. But they also had to be careful. Any clues they missed would disappear under the shopping centre.

They found things which had been used by people many hundreds of years ago and then thrown away - often on to a rubbish dump. They had to record exactly how far down they were. The further down the article was found, the older it was.

▲ **Source 1**
The builders have already begun work on the new shopping centre. Can you see the archaeologists digging at the bottom of this picture?

## What People Wore

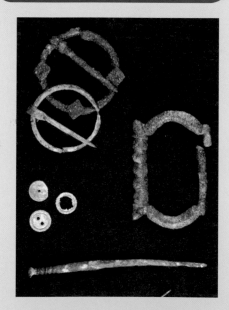

◀ **Source 2**
Turn back to page 36 and look at the women in the backland house. They are spinning and weaving thread into cloth. But the archaeologists did not find any cloth. Almost all the things people wore have rotted away. They did find the things people used to fasten their clothes. How do you think these brooches worked?

▲ **Source 3**
This comb is made from a deer's antler. Some archaeologists think it is a nit comb. How is it different from the comb you use today? Do the teeth on your comb break off like these? Why not? Do you think medieval people had coloured combs like we do today?

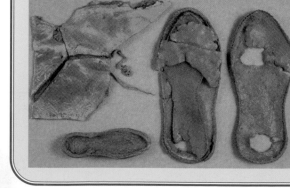

◀ **Source 4**
Look at the holes in the sole of the big shoe. What can you work out from that? The little sole must have belonged to a small child. It has no holes. Why do you think this is?

## Cooking and Eating

### ◀ Source 5

A metal pot like this was used to boil meat - usually beef. It was heated on an open fire. This pot has to stand in bumpy places. It has only three legs. Why is this better than four?

### ◀ Source 6

People ate their food from bowls like this. It is made from birch wood. It has rotted a bit while it was buried in the ground. Do you think it was healthy to eat meal after meal from a wooden bowl?

### ◀ Source 7

This pottery jug was made in Holland. Someone brought it all the way to Aberdeen, so it must have cost a lot of money. It was used to serve beer. Medieval beer was much weaker than modern beer. Most people drank beer with their meals because the water was so dirty. What happens when you drink dirty water?

Imagine you are an archaeologist in the future. You have just dug up lots of things dating from around the year 2000 AD. Draw pictures of these things (or use photographs). Perhaps you found: plastic combs, brushes and bowls; a toaster; a TV set; metal knives and forks; rubber boots; chicken bones; tins of cat or dog food, and so on. Write about your finds as if you had never seen them before. You will have to guess what they were used for. And you might just make a mistake...!

### A C T I V I T I E S

# The Monks of Melrose

If you visit Melrose Abbey today you put on headphones. You can hear a voice telling you what to look out for. Imagine that when you put the headphones on, you hear the voice of a monk from the fourteenth century. He is called Brother John. (All monks are called Brothers). He is telling you all about his life at the Abbey.

**Source 1 ▶**
This plan of the Abbey will help you follow what Brother John is doing.

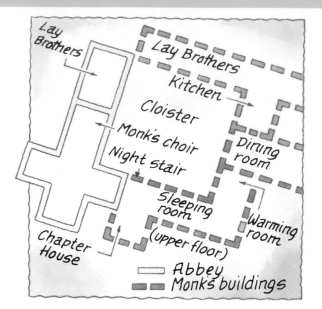

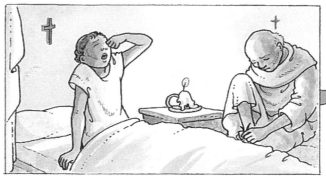

**1** My day starts at 2 a.m. The Abbey bell wakes us up. All the monks share one large sleeping room. In winter it is very dark and cold. I dress in a white woollen cloak and sandals. We walk down the night stair to the church.

**2** We all kneel in the choir places. We have six services every day. This one is the first. The most important work we do is to pray to God and to sing hymns. In the busy world outside, people have no time to worship properly.

**3** We have no breakfast. Instead, we go into the chapter house for our daily meeting. It is called the chapter house because the Abbot reads out a chapter from our rules. If I have broken a rule, I must ask to be forgiven.

**4** We also have to work with our hands. Today I work in the fields on my own. I like that. I look after the sheep or sometimes...

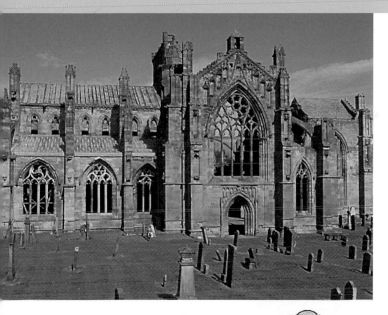

**Draw and write about your own day at school. How is it like Brother John's day? How is it different?**

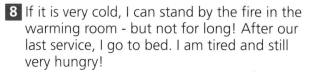

5 ... I help in the kitchen. I cannot eat any of the food we prepare. I am not allowed to speak to the other monks. It's hard! If I speak, I may have to eat just bread and water for a while.

6 We have only one meal a day. It is in the late afternoon. Usually, it is bread and cooked vegetables. We drink weak beer. We cannot talk to each other.

7 Every evening, we read in the cloisters between services. Cloisters are corridors with a roof but no sides. They are open to the air on one side. The seats are made of stone. Brrrr!

8 If it is very cold, I can stand by the fire in the warming room - but not for long! After our last service, I go to bed. I am tired and still very hungry!

# The Abbey's Sheep Farms

In the fourteenth century, other people lived at the Abbey as well as the monks. These people were called lay brothers. Lay means ordinary. The lay brothers wanted to serve God, but not as monks. They wanted to serve God with their hands. They did not go to all the services in the church. They lived in a different place in the Abbey, and they were allowed out. They looked after the Abbey's sheep farms, called granges.

The Abbey had lots of granges in the Borders. The high ground there was good for sheep. In the fourteenth century, Melrose Abbey had 15,000 sheep! This was more than almost anyone else in Europe.

▲ **Source 1**

Sheep were smaller in the fourteenth century. But they grew very good wool. Most of the time the sheep wandered on the hills. The shepherds had to make sure the sheep were safe in bad weather, and protect them from wolves. One of the shepherds is playing music to keep awake. Can you spot the sheepdog?

▼ **Source 2**

In summer, the shepherds took the sheep down to the valley. They fenced them in and cut off their wool with shears. They checked to see if any sheep were ill. Can you see the shepherd checking the sheep? What is the other person doing?

◄ **Source 3**
There were no proper roads in Scotland in the fourteenth century. Packhorses carried the Abbey's wool along tracks to Berwick or Leith. Then a ship took it over the sea to Bruges. Bruges is now in Belgium. There were so many Scottish wool ships that they had their own special place to go in Bruges.

**1** Make a picture show of a monk's day at Melrose. Work in a group. You will need: two pieces of A4 card, eight pieces of A4 paper, pencils and paint or crayons.

> **1** Put both pieces of card together. Make a cut half way down both pieces.
>
> **2** Slot the cards together in the shape of a saltire.
>
> **3** Draw and paint background pictures on four pieces of A4 paper. Stick them onto the frame.
>
> **4** Now draw four foreground scenes on four pieces of paper. Cut round the figures in your picture and stick them across the front of your background scenes. Hang your picture show up and turn it to see the different scenes.

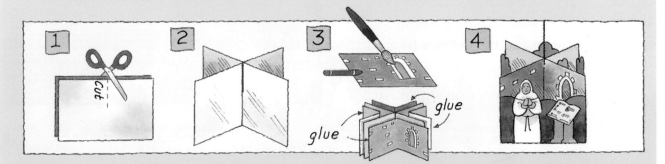

**2** Scotland still sends many things to Europe and the rest of the world. Can you think of some?

## A C T I V I T I E S

# The Highlanders

In the 14th century, Lowland Scots began to think of Highlanders as different people. John Fourdoun, who was a Lowlander, wrote this in 1380:

> *English is spoken by the people who live in the low country and on the coasts, and they are friendly, peaceful and wear decent clothes. Gaelic is spoken by the people who live in the Highlands and Islands. They are savage and untamed, wear ugly clothes, are liable to steal your goods and (although kind to friends) dislike and are cruel to people who speak English.*

▲ Source 1

Do you think this seems fair? What would the Highlanders say? Why do you think John Fourdoun said these things? Think about these points:

◆ The wars with England caused a lot of fighting among the Scots.

◆ Lowlanders saw Highlanders more often than in the past. They looked fierce.

Look at the other sources on this page before you answer.

▲ Source 2

This stone is from the grave of a Highland knight. Can you see his sword and his padded tunic? Underneath, he wore armour made of metal rings, called chainmail. His hood is also chain mail. Can you understand why Lowlanders were frightened as he rode past?

## Source 3 ▶

Stories were told of chiefs who brought their men down from the hills to burn and kill. One of the worst was called The Wolf of Badenoch. Here, John Fordoun tells us what Badenoch did in 1390.

> *With his wild, wicked Highland men he burned down the whole town of Elgin, and also (which was even more cursed) the much-loved cathedral, with all the precious things which were kept in it.*

In 1266 the Norwegians gave the Western Isles to the Scots. But the Scots were very busy fighting the English. So the islands from Lewis to Islay were really ruled by the local lords, the Macdonalds. From the 1380s, the Kings of Scots often tried to win the islands away from these Lords of the Isles.

In 1411, the Lord of the Isles tried to capture Aberdeen. He was driven off at the Battle of Harlaw. But so many men were killed there was even more hatred between the sides. In 1493 King James IV took away the title of Lord of the Isles. But it did not stop the fighting between Highlanders and Lowlanders.

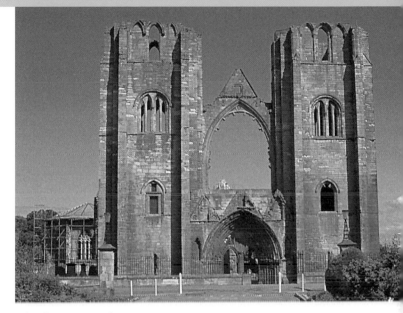

▲ **Source 4**
Elgin Cathedral is ruined again now. It probably looks like it did after the Wolf of Badenoch attacked it in 1390.

▼ **Source 5**
Urquhart Castle on Loch Ness was on a main route between the West Highlands and the Lowlands. It was sometimes captured by the Macdonalds, and sometimes by the King. It was so badly damaged that it had to be rebuilt.

1 **You are a merchant or a merchant's wife in a lowland burgh in 1400. Write a letter to a friend explaining why you fear and dislike Highlanders.**

2 **Design a display board for Urquhart Castle. Explain how the castle helps us remember the struggle between the Kings and the Lords of the Isles.**

# A C T I V I T I E S

# The Border

In the middle of the thirteenth century, England and Scotland agreed on where the border would be. It ran from the River Tweed to the Solway Firth. It is still the same today.

After all the fighting in the times of Wallace and Bruce, the English and the Scots hated each other. In 1329 King Robert died. His son, David II, was only five. He was too young to be a proper King. So King Edward III of England took his chance.

For the next 20 years he kept sending English armies into Scotland. The English ruled parts of southern Scotland. For 11 years, David was a prisoner in England.

By about 1380, the old Border was once again accepted. But that still did not end the fighting. One of Scotland's worst defeats was at Flodden on the Border in 1513. King James IV and about 30 of his lords were killed.

Many castles and towers were built on the Border because of the fighting. Some of them are still here today.

At last, the fighting on the Border began to die down in 1603, when England and Scotland got the same King. The Scots and the English now learned to live together in peace.

## Source 2 ▶
There are a lot of tower houses on the Border. This one is at Smailholm. It was built in the fifteenth century. A tower like this was too small to hold out against an army. But raiders would often come to steal cattle. People needed to take shelter in the tower houses.

▲ **Source 1**
Look at the map. Work out why the border makes a clear line. Why is it easy to defend?

▲ **Source 3**
Caerlaverock Castle was besieged by King Edward I in 1300. The English used huge catapults to throw stones at the castle and make it surrender.

**Source 4** ▶
One of the English wrote this about Caerlaverock Castle:

*It was shaped like a shield, with three sides and a tower at each corner. But one of the towers was a double one. The castle had good walls and round it were ditches full of water.*

▲ **Source 5**
Despite the siege by King Edward, Caerlaverock Castle does not look so very different today. During the fourteenth century wars it sometimes belonged to the Scots, sometimes to the English.

1 Make a display showing how castles allow us to remember the fighting on the Border. Make 3D pictures of the castles. Paint a background picture of fields or hills. Then use cardboard tubes from kitchen paper rolls for your castle towers. Cut the tubes in half lengthways and glue them on to the background.

2 If you could produce a newspaper or a TV programme in 1329 when King Robert died, what would you say? How would you report his death? What pictures would you use? What would you think of the future?

**A C T I V I T I E S**

Shetland

Orkney

*Pentland Firth*

N

Lewis

Urquhart Castle

Elgin

Buchan

Aberdeen

Scone

Dundee

Perth

St. Andrews

Iona

*Firth of Forth*

Stirling

Islay

Glasgow

Edinburgh

Largs

*River Clyde*

Berwick

Arran

Melrose

*River Tweed*

*Firth of Clyde*

**The Border**

Dumfries

*Solway Firth*